VITAL SIGNS OF VISION:

A Wellness Check for Visionary Leaders

By Bryan J. Pierce, Sr.

Vital Signs of Vision

Copyright © 2022 Bryan J. Pierce, Sr.

All rights reserved. No portion of this book may be reproduced without permission from the publisher except as permitted by U.S. copyright law. It is illegal to copy this book, post it to a website, or distribute it by any other means without permission from the publisher. For permissions, contact www.bjpministries.com.

DEDICATION

This book is dedicated to my loving wife, Debra, and our incredible children, BJ, Brandon, Devin & Bryana.

CONTENTS

INTRODUCTION 5

1. CREATIVITY 8
   Inspiration 9
   Situational 11
   Circumstance 12
   Creativity in Practice 13

2. CONTEXT 22
   Mission 26
   The "E's" 32

3. COMMUNICATION 36
   ZNN 37
   Engage Team 38
   The Habakkuk Plan 38
      Killing Goliath 39

4. COLLABORATION 50
   Administrative Leadership Is An Art 52
   Administrative Leadership Is A Science 53
   Administrative Leadership Is A Gift 53

5. COMPLETION 63

ACKNOWLEDGMENTS 71

INTRODUCTION

I was around ten years old the first time I remember my late father driving my siblings and me around the wealthy neighborhoods of New Orleans, Louisiana. We lived on the other side of town, but we would pile up in Dad's car every Sunday as he drove us through neighborhoods with lavish houses and fancy cars. I vividly remember my excitement, as it caused me to envision myself one day living in that kind of world. Even at a young age, I had a big imagination with solid plans for my future, which I later realized were early signs of being a visionary. The older I got, I began to notice the trend that God would give me vision and strategy, and as long as I stayed on his planned path, things manifested. From traveling the country on stage plays to being part of the Stellar Award-winning national recording artist *Men of Standard*, all of it began with a vision.

It was in my late 20s that God expanded my vision from myself and my family to leading a mid-size church in North Carolina. I will be the first to admit that I did not know everything there was to know about being a senior pastor, but I possessed the key to success in leadership, which is *vision*. Now, over 20 years later, I am both the senior pastor and chief executive officer of a North Carolina megachurch that annually generates multimillions in revenue and serves thousands locally, domestically, and internationally. Yet even in leading a church of this magnitude, *vision* is still the key to my success.

While my God-given vision has impacted my personal and professional life, it also echoes beyond the four walls of the church into communities and across racial, age, and cultural boundaries. And while I know what it feels like to navigate a God-given vision, I also know what it feels like to have a vision that exceeds my capacity to contain it or not understand what God is doing.

Proverbs 29:18 says that if people can't see what God is doing, they stumble all over themselves. I have been there before, and let me be the first to say that a lack of sight is not the only thing that makes people stumble. Some people have all the vision in the world but still stumble because there is no strategy, system, sequence, or structure, all of which are vital signs of vision.

Vital signs detect and monitor how well something is functioning. They serve as a compass, guiding recovery plans and wisdom on avoiding adverse effects. Irregularities in vital signs can lead practitioners to detect infections, the effectiveness of medications, and underlying conditions. In other words, vital signs provide a snapshot of our well-being — empowering lifestyle changes, preventing misdiagnoses, and encouraging us to make better overall choices.

In the same way, vital signs provide a snapshot of our well-being; vital signs can also gauge the strength and weakness of our vision. Now, if you are reading this book, you are a visionary. Perhaps you are a pastor, a business professional, or even an entrepreneur trying to figure out the next steps for vision in your context. Let me go ahead and tell you that you have come to the right place. In the chapters of this book, I share my blueprint to success with vision-casting and execution, including paying off a multi-million-dollar facility in four years, re-branding an organization, and traversing through tradition to modernize organizational culture. Through every leadership and ministry success, there were five vital signs of vision that I always kept at the forefront: creativity, context, communication, collaboration, and completion. In this book, I candidly expand on these vital signs from my experience. While many of my examples will be church-related, they can be applied to any organizational context. While serving as a "how to" guide for leaders to execute a vision successfully, this book will empower and challenge you beyond your comfort zone to cultivate and execute a vision in your organization, company, or church. So go ahead and lean in; it's time to take a deep dive into the vital signs of vision.

Chapter 1:
CREATIVITY

Creativity is a process of generating new ideas or ways of doing things. It involves seeing things in new ways, thinking outside the box, and finding new solutions to problems. Creativity is often associated with the arts but is not limited to them. It can be found in all areas of life, from solving everyday problems to running our businesses.

For me, creativity is my automatic response to problem-solving. When a problem arises, my creativity is sparked. It has been this way since I was a kid playing football in the streets. First, my friends and I did not have a football field, so we created one in the street. Then that summer, my friends and I were really into wrestling. We used cardboard boxes to create championship belts and made a makeshift wrestling ring with hose pipes, ropes, sticks, buckets, and any other tool we could use. Oh, and then there was that time we made our scooters out of wood and roller skate wheels. I could go on and on, but the bottom line is that my creativity always went into overdrive when faced with a problem.

I suppose that is why even as an adult, that same creativity has followed me into the professional world. When traversing situations and problems, it is my natural response to step up to challenges through creativity. Outside of problem-solving, there are many ways to encourage creativity. One is to provide opportunities for people to explore their imagination and develop new ideas through brainstorming sessions. Another way is to create an environment conducive to creativity, such as a workplace encouraging risk-taking and innovation. Whatever the approach, fostering creativity can positively impact individuals, businesses, and society. Creativity is not cookie-cutter. Instead, your creativity lives somewhere near your inspiration. So again, I ask: what inspires your creativity?

Inspiration

According to the Merriam-Webster dictionary, inspiration is "the act or power of causing someone to have new ideas or a better opinion of something: the act or power of inspiring someone." In other words, inspiration drives us to create or do something new. It can be found in minor things, like a child's smile, or the largest, like a painting by Vincent van Gogh. Inspiration is everywhere if we only take the time to look for it. And when we find it, it has the power to change our lives forever.

Inspiration is the first step in discovering or revealing your creativity, which is why I keep this question at the forefront of this chapter. It is essential to figure out what stimulates your creativity and gets your creative juices flowing. To answer this question, you may find yourself switching up your routine, taking time to rest, or simply paying closer attention to the moments you feel most motivated. In a study on the creative process, researchers found that "inspiration is not posited to be the source of creative ideas. Instead, inspiration is a motivational response to creative ideas. Thus, inspiration explains the transmission, not the origin, of creativity" (2014, Oleynick, Thrash, LeFew, Moldovan, & Kieffaber). In other words, we communicate what inspires us through creativity, making creativity fluid and far-reaching. Yet how often do we skip over creativity when executing vision because we say, "Oh, I'm not creative" or "I'll leave the creative part to someone else." I would solicit any visionary to be reminded that you will never discover your creativity if you continue to devalue it or if you consistently feel undeserving of that truth!

Despite success in their field, many people feel like imposters and not supposed to be where they are. Those who constantly doubt their abilities and fear being exposed in their work as fraud are said to have imposter syndrome. This imposter syndrome can be debilitating, making people doubt their abilities and accomplishments. It can be especially prevalent among women and minorities, who may feel they must work twice as hard to be taken seriously.

I would even go as far as to say that some leaders fail to tap into their creativity for fear of being scrutinized or challenged on their gifting and being "found out." But to be a great leader, you must face imposter syndrome head-on, as it is something that can be overcome with awareness and effort. Recognizing the signs of imposter syndrome is the first step. If you find yourself constantly doubting your abilities or feeling like a fraud, it may be time to seek help from a therapist or counselor. Once you understand the source of your doubts, you can start to address them head-on. Overcoming imposter syndrome and building confidence in your skills and accomplishments is possible with time and effort.

Situational

Another way to discover your creativity is through situations out of your control. Take the global pandemic, for example. Every professional and business owner was forced to reset, recreate, and recalibrate to function. As a result, everything in our lives changed — from the way we did family to school and church. Specifically, in what felt like an overnight jolt, pastors across the country were forced to become creatives as they embodied makeshift software engineers and media techs in their pursuit to keep parishioners connected to the worship experience.

It is far from ironic that six years before the pandemic, God gave me a vision for iChurch. iChurch is a virtual campus that connects members, guests, and friends to our weekly worship experiences. Furthermore, God blessed me with a capable and passionate team pastor who was ready and willing to take my iChurch vision and bring it to pass. With this in mind, when the pandemic came and everything shut down, we already had the infrastructure to keep our members engaged and connected to the Sunday and Wednesday worship experiences. However, the situation of the pandemic did lead me to be more creative through safety protocols, such as rethinking in-person meetings with my staff, putting programming online so people could still serve the ministry and even community service, and turning events into drive-throughs so we could still serve the least, the left out and the lonely.

Circumstance

God will use circumstances to help you discover your creativity. I know this because God speaks to me through circumstances, problem-solving, and conflict. When considering the circumstances of your business, you pay close attention to the conditions at play, such as financial, societal, political, technological, and even ethical. The abundance or lack thereof in any of these conditions can inspire your creativity.

I recall being in small talk with a pastor colleague who was giving my church kudos. Amid the compliment, he said, "Man, if I had half of what you had, I could do so much more with my congregation!" I let him finish talking but soon came back to his comment. I reminded him that where I am is not where I started, and I shared with him that his circumstances should not foster a sense of lack but instead inspire creativity. Instead of wishing he "had what I had," I encouraged him to think out of the box right where he was. So no, maybe feeding 1,000 people in one giveaway was unrealistic for his context, but he could partner with a community organization and feed 200, which would still make a real impact. Perhaps he did not have the budget to purchase thousands in technology equipment, but why not be creative and see how to use what he had better? In other words, as leaders, circumstances should inspire us, not limit us.

There is a danger in overlooking our circumstances and lingering on others. Not only can it birth jealousy and envy, but it can cause one to be blind to their assignment. For example, years ago, I attended a conference at which Bishop T.D Jakes was ministering to a group of pastors. During the session, he said something I will never forget, "If I throw you the keys to my church, don't catch them." In other words, he said, don't get so caught up in how grand something looks because (1) you don't know what it takes to manage and maintain it, and (2) never overlook the value of your own circumstance. Sometimes, you have to get creative.

Creativity in Practice

My creativity comes from a heart of evangelism. I not only want to share God with the world, but I always desire to do it in a way that is authentic, refreshing, and new! In that vein, I am a creative. To be labeled a creative suggests a person is original, authentic, or even artistic, or that one can dive deep into their imagination to produce unique expressions in the workplace. This term is a vital sign of vision as it often deals with how vision is packaged. So, let me ask, are you a creative? The answer is YES! While, at first glance, it may appear far-fetched from the way you identify yourself, I would posit that since we are all created by a creative God, we are all creatives. Just think, God took a blank canvas and created the moon, stars, water, forest, mountains, and animals. Even now, look around you. Every single detail was handcrafted and methodically thought through by our Savior. That is both divine and creative. And because you and I possess the creativity from our Father, we must use this gift to re-imagine our churches, companies, and organizations.

Many business leaders will be voted or hired into our leadership positions. In this process, we inherit modes of tradition, especially when it comes to programming. In the context of a church, many Baptist pastors inherit:

- Women's Day and Men's Day
- Family and Friends Day
- Volunteers

While these special days and programs are essential to some congregation members, they are steeped in tradition, which can also come with antiquated biases. How do you know if there are traditional biases toward your programming or volunteer structure? Here are a few signs:

- Lack of growth
- Lack of excitement
- Lack of clear structure

Does this sound familiar? If so, it could be time to tap into your creativity. In other words, I am not encouraging you to discard programming birthed out of tradition; I am encouraging you to develop and re-present it. In other words, demonstrate your gift of creativity. I am blessed to pastor an incredible church that is 122 years old. There is so much rich history and valuable tradition that I would not dare discard the hard work of my predecessors. So instead, I took some of the more traditional areas and used my gift of creativity to manifest the vision God gave me. So lean into the following pages as I go deeper into this thought and show how creativity can impact your organization, even using language and names.

Imagine Kingdom. I led a re-design of the children's church. This re-design was both contextual and creative as it was a complete revamp of the space and program. In this restructuring, God led me to re-brand the area "Imagine Kingdom," a space that sparked the use of imagination, creativity, and invention as the kids learned about Christ. I stood before my congregation at the ribbon cutting of this completed space. I said, "We will call this new space *Imagine Kingdom* because the most powerful nation is our imagination!" At that moment, I did not even understand the full magnitude of that phrase. Since then, God has had me revisit it many times and re-present it in sermons and speeches as I challenge people to tap into their imagination and creativity to make visions come to pass.

When choosing the name of our children's re-design, I wanted to marry the idea of the Magic Kingdom at Disney World to imagining the Kingdom of God. Proverbs 23:7a says, "For as he thinketh in his heart, so is he." Knowing the importance of the formative K-5 years, I wanted to create a fantasy-focused space where kids could imagine what it was like to be part of God's kingdom.

At the time of the revamp, our church used the word "Kingdom" in much of our vocabulary. From sermons to themes, such as "kingdom structure," the word was in our everyday vocabulary. So as I prayed for a new name for our children's space, God married all of these ideas and gave me, "Imagine Kingdom." To this day, the name still excites me as I know this is a space where kids begin to find language in creating their relationship with Christ. It is a space for them to tell their own story, a place where evangelism beings.

Family Matters Month. Like some of you reading this book, I grew up in a church celebrating Family and Friends Day yearly. As the name suggests, this was a special Sunday when the congregation was encouraged to bring friends and family to church. The pastor would preach a message about family, and there would be a repass following service. I love the idea of bringing family together. My wife heard from God at our first pastoral ministry assignment to birth Family Matters, something for the family that was much more than a one-day celebration, but a conference built to empower the entire family. Let me be honest: while the vision was clear, that particular church context was not a good fit for the manifestation of the vision. Let this be an encouragement to anyone with a vision that did not work the first time or did not carry the weight you thought it would. That vision still has value and power; it may just need to be developed. Fast-forward to when God transitioned me into my current ministry assignment. That weekend conference soon became a whole month of empowerment events for the entire family, now called Family Matters Month. Throughout Family Matters Month, every Sunday is dedicated to preaching on different aspects of the family while offering engaging family-centered events. The events are just as creative as the sermon series and while they shift every year, below are some of our most popular Family Matters events:

- Couples Garden Party
- Men's Retreat
- Women's Paint Party
- Movie on the Lawn
- College Cookout

The events are filled with excitement and offered for free or at a nominal cost. I know you may be saying, "Well, my organization's budget does not allow me to do ALL of that." If you're saying that, you are missing the point. The value of the events is not in quantity but the creativity; it's about offering something to your demographic that is fresh and fun. We also do things to add a buzz to Family Matters Month, including bringing out food trucks after the Sunday worship experience and encouraging people to purchase their food and hang out after service.

Killing Goliath. The story of David and Goliath is taught across denominations, from vacation Bible school to Sunday school. It is a familiar topic that resonates with the "underdog." From a pastoral and leadership perspective, this story is a natural go-to when it comes to empowering your audience in the areas of courage, dedication, and bravery.

Just in case you are reading this book and the story is unfamiliar, I encourage you to read 1 Samuel 17, where you will find the story of a little shepherd boy, David, winning in battle against Goliath, a terrifying giant. David's faith in a battle allowed him to conquer a giant so much bigger than he; David was positioned to fail, but God not only kept him in battle but allowed him to be victorious over the enemy.

As a preacher, I cannot tell you how many times I have preached on the story of David and Goliath. Let's say enough for me to be *familiar* with the text. Yet my imagination caused me to take this biblical story and turn it into an entire debt-elimination campaign, Killing Goliath. Our church paid off over $5 million of pre-existing debt during this campaign in four years. The truth is if I had called the campaign "Pay Off Debt Fund" or "Let's Pay Off the Church," that would not have been captivating or relatable to anyone. But when I titled the campaign "Killing Goliath," that was a name everyone could get on board with and was passionate about because we ALL want to kill Goliath. With this in mind, get creative with your campaign names, and remember to make them relatable to your audience.

Dream Team. Any sports fan will tell you that "Dream Team" is used when a single group or team comprises the best players. While it is often used in the context of sports teams, I brought this term into the culture of my church to describe the volunteers. I intended to re-present volunteering as something that evoked pride and excitement. The volunteers do much of the heavy lifting each week and are the Dream Team!

This name change added a new level of excitement to the volunteer experience, along with pride in serving. It's been 5-6 years since that name change, and since that time, we now have a Pastor of Dream Team, Dream Teamer of the Quarter, Dream Team Night, and even Dream Team T-shirts. We've branded Dream Team as something that members want to join.

In addition to re-branding and changing the names of facets of your organization, I encourage you to "think outside of the box." Get creative even with everyday tasks and programming. I use creativity as a problem-solving tool that gives me the flexibility to reach more people. When you problem-solve through the lens of creativity, you will find yourself using innovation and exploring open-ended solutions within your context.

NOTES

NOTES

Chapter 2:
CONTEXT

Outside of my pastoral duties, I am graced to preach, teach, and facilitate at conferences and ministries across the country. And while I take necessary sabbaths, the truth remains that I spend a lot of time telling people about Jesus. Of course, in doing this, I rely on the Bible, and I coined a phrase at the top of most of my sermons and teachings in which I say, "Scriptures are always better understood in context." I am saying that Scriptures are always misunderstood outside of context. Would you agree? And if we agree with that truth, it should be no surprise that the same applies to *vision*. When there is no context for vision, it will be misunderstood, for context is the bed for your vision to lay. So here is the first question you must ask yourself: When casting vision, what and who is my context? In other words, where does your vision fit within your organization?

Context is everything. The environment in which something is experienced can profoundly affect its meaning and impact. For example, a text read in school might be seen as dry and uninteresting, but the exact text read for pleasure might be seen as intriguing and thought-provoking. A work of art viewed in a museum might be appreciated for its beauty, but the same work viewed in a public space might provoke anger or disgust. Context is what gives us the ability to see things in new ways and to find meaning in our experiences. Without it, our world would be much poorer.

After receiving a vision and gaining clarity from God, my next stop is always meeting with church leaders for context. Church leaders include an Elder's Council, executive staff, pastoral team, and over 30 ministry leaders. The context I provide to my team of leaders for vision can come from provided scriptures or even proven success stories. Moreover, I make sure to align my God-given vision with a permanent contextual space, whether it be our strategic plan, yearly theme, or even themed months. So let's take a closer look at what the implementation of this alignment looks like in my context.

In the last chapter, I told you how the name change from Volunteer Ministry to Dream Team came to be, but there is a contextual part of this transformation that deserves elaboration. As God gave me the name Dream Team and all of the faculties therein, I knew I could not just show up in the pulpit one day calling the head usher a "Dream Teamer." Can you imagine the confusing looks I would have gotten? I also knew I could not attend the next meeting with my executive staff, saying, "From this day forward, all volunteers are Dream Teamers." So instead, I clarified my context, and once I was clear on what God was sharing with me about our volunteers, I took the idea to my church leaders, shared with them the God-given vision of a Dream Team, and showed them the context in which the vision fit. This gave way not only to expanding the idea of Dream Team but to us now having a Dream Team pastor, a Dream Team Month, and even a Dream Team Night where we celebrate every person who volunteers at our church. Now our Dream Team is an intricate part of our culture, with designated T-shirts and a genuine pride for people to participate in the volunteer efforts of the church.

Another part of our strategic plan is planting. Our church is 122 years strong and a pillar of our community. Part of the vision God gave me for our church was to have a multi-site. But again, I did not get the vision and casually announce it from the pulpit. Instead, I ensured the vision informed the strategic plan and combed through it with my church leaders. In other words, I am intentional about not only hearing from God but clarifying my context before presenting it to my leadership team.

Now I know what you are saying: "If you are the senior pastor and CEO, why do you run a God-given vision through so many people? What you say should go!" Let me caution you here by sharing that having a wise and God-fearing team of leaders to run vision and ideas past is pertinent. It is obsolete to assume that once a leader has a vision, they should keep it to themselves, announce it over the mic one Sunday, and expect the congregation to "go with it." That is both outdated and out of order. Instead, I challenge every leader to surround themselves with a team they can trust and from whom they can receive feedback. This does not negate your leadership; it strengthens it!

When God surrounds you with a team of leaders with whom you can sit down and present a God-given vision that aligns with the organization's context before executing it- that is excellence! Don't get me wrong; it takes a lot of research because I do not just hear from God and run with it. After hearing clearly from God, I do my research to ensure that I present the vision to my team. In those closed-door meetings, the most challenging questions are asked, and I can work through strategy and implementation. Presenting it at many levels before hitting the congregation is more for my covering and benefit than anyone else. Think of it like this if I can answer the hard questions behind the scenes, I am better prepared to articulate the idea in public. Why wait until a church meeting or public forum to be overwhelmed with questions that you may or may not be prepared to answer? Instead, have those hard conversations in advance to prepare yourself and gain allies who support the vision. There are also parts of leadership that are lonely for anyone, but that doesn't account for every part of it. When you can gain allies, generate support for the vision God has given you within your context.

Now perhaps your context is not clear. Maybe there is not a strategic plan in place or a clearly defined space where your vision "neatly' fits in your organizational structure. Whenever there is no context, let faith become your context; contextualize your vision by faith. In this vein, when there is no previous reference point, you must be a trailblazer and lean into Proverbs 3:6 (NKJV), which says, "in all your ways acknowledge Him, and He shall direct your paths." This is the transformative space where you become the headlight, not the tail lights! And catch this, headlights not only bring clarity, but most in this day and age are made from polycarbonate plastic. This is a strong plastic known for taking on severe road conditions. In the same way, as God gives you a headlight grace for your vision, He equips you to traverse even the most challenging conditions you may face. So instead of being worried about not having a context, lean into your faith. As you lean into your faith, you will clarify your context. To do this, ask yourself questions like (1) Who gave you the vision and (2) from where did the vision come? Now let me go ahead and give you a heads up: if your vision came from God, you must be comfortable with not everyone understanding it.

Sometimes, God gives you a vision not understood by others simply because He gave the vision to YOU. While it can feel agonizing, the truth is that sometimes God will give you a vision for which you have no context because HE wants you to be the first to do it! Doesn't that sound like our God? Just think: at creation, there was no context for man, woman, animals, night, or day; God was the first to do it. And throughout history, there are several men and women to whom God has given vision with no context. Lean in for a moment and reflect on Garrett Morgan, who created the three-light traffic signal; Frederick Jones, who created refrigerated trucks, Alexander Miles, who created automatic elevator doors; Lewis Lamiter, who invented the carbon light bulb filament; and, of course, Madam CJ Walker who invented the world's first hair-straightening formula and the hot comb. God did not give context to their vision; instead, he gave each person the lens to view a problem with a solution in the form of a vision; in other words, they were the first to ever do it! So as you consider your vision and whether it fits into context or if you are the first to ever do it, I want to provide a few examples of context that I use to align vision effectively. Let's start with our mission.

Mission

A mission statement briefly describes an organization's purpose, priorities, and values. It is typically used as a guide for decision-making and strategic planning. A mission statement should be clear and concise and summarize the essence of what the organization does and why it exists. It should also be realistic and achievable. An effective mission statement can help to focus an organization's efforts and ensure everyone is working towards the same goals. It can also help communicate with stakeholders and the public. When writing a mission statement, it is essential to consider what the organization hopes to achieve and who its target audience is.

At Mount Zion, our mission statement is "[t]o reconcile the world to God through Jesus Christ." In other words, we want to bring unsaved souls in the world to Christ. This serves as the context for our actions because it is at the core of our programming, events, and worship experiences. As new ideas and innovative opportunities are presented, we continually revisit our mission statement, allowing it to be the baseline from which vision is launched. Take, for example, our Serve The City movements, which are our community outreach efforts. They fall within the context of our mission because whether we are doing a gas giveaway, bike giveaway, or providing financial support for those in need, our purpose is always to reach souls and bring them to Jesus Christ.

Theme Months

Every month, my church has a dedicated theme within which all sermons, events, and teachings fall. First, I will list the themes we use each month at a high level. Then, I will detail how each theme impacts worship and programming. As I always say, be sure to "eat the fish and spit out the bones" as you consider if this context is appropriate for your ministry or organization setting.

- January: Vision Month
- February: Stewardship Month
- March: Pastor's Anniversary Month
- April: No Greater Love
- May: Prayer Month
- June: Open
- July" Rest Month
- August: Family Matters Month
- September: Discipleship Month
- October: Teamgelism Month
- November: Dream Team Month
- Rest Month

Every January is Vision Month and is used to cast vision for the year ahead. During this time, I meet with over 150 leaders of the church in a corporate setting as we take a deep dive into the vision for the year., I also facilitate our once-a-year full-body church meeting this month, which we call vision casting. This brings together leaders and parishioners as we vote on the church budget and review ministry reports. Now let me add this tidbit: one of the changes I made post-pandemic was that all reports are pre-recorded and shown during the church meeting. This helped streamline the church meeting and provided optimal clarity on all topics (vs. reports given on a mic). In the first month of the year, there is also a 20-40 day fasting period, which I find essential as the church body postures itself to receive a fresh vision.

February is all about stewardship. However, instead of focusing solely on the financial aspects of it, we also hit on stewardship of time and talent. During the first sermon of the series, I provide a definition that remains our baseline for the entire month. I preach on this topic every Sunday but do so in a way that doesn't *beat them over the head* and empowers them to give their *time*, *talent*, and *tithe*. This is also a great time to bring guest speakers in during mid-week services. For this, we've had a range of speakers, including banking professionals and home-buying experts. One of my favorite guests during Stewardship Month was Dr. DeForest Soaries, Jr., whose candid dialogue on debt elimination and building wealth empowered our congregation. Now Dr. Soaries also happened to have a debt elimination program called dfree Lifestyle which took many people in our congregation through a plan to get out of debt. We created a small group called Kingdom Groups, where people could sign up to go through the plan together. So our primary goal for Stewardship Month is to normalize stewardship in the lives of our congregation.

March is Pastor's Celebration Month and truly one of the most humbling months for my family and me. During this month, gifts are given to the pastor and family to celebrate the blessing and sacrifice of serving in leadership.

April is reserved for No Greater Love! This month is focused on our church being the hands and feet of Jesus by showing the community that there is no love greater than Jesus Christ. With Easter kicking off this month, we have a churchwide theatrical production on Sunday re-enacting the crucifixion. Then we offer community events throughout the month, including outdoor baptisms, food giveaways, and gas giveaways. We are intentional about serving communities that are in underserved areas, such as food deserts and government-funded housing.

May is Prayer Month, a powerful month filled with opportunities to bring people together for prayer. We do this differently every year, including a mid-day National Day of Prayer Service, 5 a.m. prayer services, midnight prayers, and ministry-specific prayer programming, including:

- ✧ When Women Pray: A breakfast brunch for women to pray
- ✧ The Prayer Cave: An evening when men come together to pray

Throughout Prayer Month, we also have a host of guests join us for midweek services giving insight into prayer. This year, God gave me a vision for a nine-week churchwide corporate prayer service that happened every Saturday at 5 a.m. Hundreds of people came out and experienced the overwhelming presence of God every week.

June is an open month that is not specific to a theme as ministries wind down to prepare for Rest Month in July. July is reserved for Rest Month, a month of rest and rejuvenation, as we put all church events on a sabbath.

August is Family Matters Month, where we cater to the entire family. Each Sunday is aligned with a theme, Women's Sunday, Men's Sunday, etc., and exciting events throughout the month bring together the entire family. Family Matters events range from movie nights for the family, off-campus bowling for men, paint parties for women, and even garden parties for couples. This is also a month in which we bring in guest preachers who bring extra excitement to the month. After the excitement of Family Matters, we shift gears to slow walk through Discipleship Month.

September is Discipleship Month, and I always start the month by sharing with the congregation that the sermons are poised as insightful conversations versus charismatic sermons. There is a place in ministry to "shout" the people, but as a leader, I am also responsible for intentionally moving slower through specific topics, such as discipleship. I don't want to shout people through the month and take the chance of them missing one of the most critical aspects of Christianity, bringing souls to Christ. Now, this is no "lifeless" month, as it is still exciting as congregants are empowered with the tools and resources to bring souls to Christ.

October is filled with excitement as we dive into Teamgelism, our take on Evangelism. Each Sunday, the congregation is encouraged to bring to church members of their team, which include family members and work friends. We even have a Sunday where our congregation comes decked out in their favorite team attire! The energy is fun, and we shed light on the importance of spreading the good news of Jesus to the world!

November's theme is Dream Team Month. Being a Dream Teamer at Mount Zion gives you access to an entire month of celebrating your service to the church. The most remarkable aspect of this month is the Dream Team Night, in which we honor our Dream Teamer of the Year and other superlatives purposed to honor and celebrate those who are genuinely at the heart of what we do at Mount Zion. This night always includes special guests, good music, and great food!

December is Rest Month, but there is something extraordinary that we did for the first time in 2021 called *Christmas at Zion*. On the Sunday leading up to Christmas, instead of a traditional sermon, we used our time and resources to demonstrate the love of Jesus LIVE during a morning worship experience through generous giving. We paid off student loans, gave away cars, blessed widows, and gave financial gifts to several families who found themselves in need. As we gave during service, the congregation exploded in worship and excitement as we thanked God for the opportunity to give liberally and freely! That Sunday, we gave over $1 million away. Indeed, that is an electrifying experience that reminded us of the reason for the season!

The "E's"

Ministries at Mount Zion are organized under one of the following *E's*: Exaltation, Evangelism, Equipping, Encouragement, and Enabling. This ministry structure lays a framework for how our ministries function, grouping ministries with shared goals. It also provides a context for vision in that much of our programming can fit within one of these categories.

Strategic Plan

Strategic planning is a powerful strategy for aligning vision. A strategic plan is a document that articulates an organization's goals, values, and objectives. It also outlines the strategies and tactics that will be used to achieve those goals. In short, a strategic plan is a road map for success. The first step in creating a strategic plan is to conduct a SWOT analysis. SWOT stands for strengths, weaknesses, opportunities, and threats. Once the SWOT analysis is complete, the next step is to set goals. These goals should be specific, measurable, achievable, relevant, and time-bound. After the goals have been set, developing strategies and tactics to help achieve them is crucial. Finally, the last step is to create an action plan. This should include a timeline and assign responsibility for each task. Following these steps, you can develop a comprehensive strategic plan to help your organization achieve its objectives.

At Mount Zion, we have a strategic planning team that, alongside me, creates the church's strategic plan every five years. The vision God gives me informs our strategic plan, and goals and objectives are established to see the vision through. Because God readily gives fresh vision, we remain flexible and update the strategic plan every five years. For example, even though Killing Goliath was not implemented until 2015, I shared this vision with the strategic planning team in 2012. Thus, during the three years, objectives were set to clearly outline our goal of debt elimination.

NOTES

NOTES

Chapter 3:
COMMUNICATION

As a leader, it is vital to communicate your vision to the people who work for you. After all, they are the ones who will be responsible for bringing your vision to life. The first step is to develop a clear and concise statement of your vision. This should articulate what you hope to achieve and why it is important. Once you have developed your vision statement, you must find ways to share it with your team. This may involve holding regular meetings, sending out memos or emails, or posting them in a visible location. Whatever method you choose, it is crucial that everyone on your team understands your vision and is committed to achieving it. With a clear and shared vision, you will be well on your way to success.

Paul Watzlawick, an Austrian communication expert, once said, "You cannot not communicate." In other words, he was saying that it is in our human nature to communicate, whether we do it well or poorly. Think of it like this: someone gets upset with you and ignores you. They may not use words, but they communicate their dismay through silence. Or even a child too young to form sentences, through actions and random words, they let their parents know their likes and dislikes. In this same vein, it is your and my responsibility to community clearly with those in and outside our organization.

As I shared in the last chapter, I do a lot of communication before I even launch into vision. I have boardroom meetings, do a lot of research, and have a lot of people combing through a vision before it is executed. Such information must be shared with our intergenerational membership as a large organization. With this in mind, I will spend the following pages sharing ways we communicate in my context.

ZNN

In my current ministry context, there are over 50 ministries and over 100 worship experiences and programs/events. That alone is a mouthful of details and registrations on a monthly, if not weekly, basis. In addition, there is always a new event or special meeting to be communicated. While the church website and bulletin were ways to communicate, I was specifically seeking a way to prioritize and communicate at a high level the events and programs that were most pressing when I felt I had the most significant attention from the congregation, Sunday mornings. From this search came Zion News Network, or as we call it, ZNN. ZNN is a pre-recorded video that shows during service, highlighting the events and registrations for the coming week. The video lasts between 3-5 minutes. We branded both with the ZNN logo and entrance music, so when the music plays and the sanctuary lights dim, our congregation knows to turn their attention to the screens. While ZNN continues to be a fun and energizing way to keep our congregation informed, we opened ourselves to a new hurdle: our members who had questions about ZNN or online registrations. That is where the Engage Center came into play.

Engage Team

The Engage Team is likened to our customer service team, and I cannot reiterate enough how invaluable a well-informed team service team is. This fun group of men and women is strategically placed at campus entry points. Using mobile desks branded with the "Engage" logo, which we call Engage Centers, the Engage is equipped to answer questions about any event or program shown on ZNN. Additionally, Square registers allow people to pay for registrations or merchandise in person versus online (we promote online purchases, but we want to meet those who are not so comfortable purchasing online). The most significant part is having a trained team to answer questions, point you in the right direction or tie any loose ends or misconceptions. We also use the Engage Center as a meeting spot for guests and large groups visiting campus. We'll say, "Meet at the Engage Center as you enter the building," and there, we will have someone in place to greet them and take them to their seats.

The Habakkuk Plan

While ZNN and Engage are how we communicate programming and announcements weekly, communicating vision requires a higher level of strategy. God gave me a strategy for communicating vision by helping me focus on content.

Within every God-given vision, there is *content*. Content refers to what is included inside something. Thus, before a vision is executed, you must examine and clarify the content therein. In other words, who and or what makes up the vision? Perhaps the answer to this is plain for you, but for those pausing to find an answer, I invite you to use the Principles from the Habakkuk Plan.

In Habakkuk 2:2-3, God lays out what I call "Principles from the Habakkuk Plan." While some people may read this text as a simple prompting to write down a vision, I see it as a much broader three-point plan for clarifying its content. Below are the three principles of the plan that I see in the text mentioned above:

- ❖ Principle 1: Write It
- ❖ Principle: Make It Plain
- ❖ Principle 3: Place It Where Others Can Read It

These three principles are at the core of the strategy God gave me for Killing Goliath, a multi-million-dollar debt-payoff campaign over four years. More specifically, Killing Goliath was an assignment from God to eliminate over $5 million of debt on our campus. Yes, I know, some people would call that "good debt," but the goal was to pay it off, allowing us to leave a legacy of being a debt debt-free church and campus to future generations.

Killing Goliath.

Early in pastoral ministry at my current church, God gave me the vision for Killing Goliath. What started as a sermon transformed into something much bigger, a strategy for eliminating five million dollars of pre-existing debt on the church. As I sought clarity on this vision from God, I found myself using principles from the Habakkuk Plan to comb through the content and identify exactly what this vision entailed. I took out a piece of paper and asked myself the following questions:

1. What is the vision?
2. Why should we do it?
3. Who will benefit from the vision?
4. How can I involve the congregation in carrying out this vision?

I soon realized that catching a God-given vision was one thing, but being able to meticulously pull out the content was a whole other giant. Yet God's faithfulness answered each of my questions so I could communicate clearly to my leaders and the congregation.

Principle 1: Write It

As God gave me clarity about Killing Goliath, I communicated with precision to ensure that I left no rock unturned as I laid out this plan on how we would pay off this enormous debt. This is where explaining the content of the vision was of utmost importance. I knew I could not share a vision of this magnitude without explaining how it would directly impact our members. Questions I knew I would need to answer included: What does this mean for the church? Will you be calling for additional offerings every Sunday? Will we have to cut out church events until after we pay it off? And why exactly are we paying it off? Knowing some common questions that might arise, I took my first leadership meeting of 2015 to cast vision and debunk theories or questions that would thwart the vision.

Principle: Make It Plain

I learned a long time ago in ministry that if I can debunk questions upfront, I disarm some of my greatest voices of opposition. To debunk is to expose or demystify a thing, meaning that it was my responsibility to present the vision in a way that countered conceivable disapproval; in other words, it was my responsibility to *make it plain*. In keeping with my leadership model, I started the conversation about Killing Goliath with my leaders. In these meetings, I leaned on my team member's strengths to help me articulate the content of the vision. Some of the strengths I pulled on include:

- ◇ Chief financial officer: Using their gift of accounting and finance to provide a clear picture of the church's financial standing and how we could achieve this significant goal.
- ◇ Chief administrative officer: Worked through the plan of how we would be the best stewards over day-to-day ministry spending to preserve the church budget.
- ◇ Strategic Planning Team: Helped to show how this vision aligned with the current strategic plan.
- ◇ Administrative support and marketing: Created PowerPoints and handouts that were visually appealing, and informative.
- ◇ Accounting Team: Created a process in our data entry system to manage and update donations.

Many other gifts were used to pull the content out of this vision, but I hope you see the time and research that went into pulling the content out of this vision. Content takes time, research, and in-depth exploration of your organization's past, present, and future. Grabbing the content from the vision and packaging it so people could understand and rally behind it was essential. From those meetings, below is the content my leaders and I pulled from the Killing Goliath vision:

1. **What is it?** It is a debt-elimination plan to retire the remaining debt of our sanctuary early. It is under the banner of our 20/20 Vision which allows us to refocus our resources and renew our vision for the future.

2. **Why are we doing it?** So that we can continue to move forward with God's mission and plan for Mount Zion, which includes family enrichment, community development, evangelism, outreach, and local and global church planting.

3. **Who will benefit from this?** Our families, children, seniors, community, and ultimately the Kingdom of God.

4. **How can you get involved?** Visit our website, www.mtzbc.com, and look for the Lifetime Stewardship banner.

My team took the content above, placed it in quarters on a sheet of paper, and handed it out at our January 2015 leadership meeting, where I first presented Killing Goliath to over 150 leaders of Mount Zion. Now, remember, at the time of this presentation, the vision had already gone through my leaders, so it had been vetted by those who work closest to me.

When presenting the plan, I provided context, showing how Killing Goliath aligned directly with the objectives in our strategic plan and the benefit of the legacy it would leave for generations to come. I could answer so many questions before they were even asked by emphasizing the content of the vision. I will never forget the claps and cheers that rang throughout the meeting room as over 150 leaders stood in agreement on this God-given vision.

The following week, our church held Vision Casting, our annual churchwide full-body meeting. As I introduced Killing Goliath, my team passed out the quarter sheets detailing the content of the vision and how it would impact each of them. Attendees were told that they would have the opportunity to align their support with a financial gift the next day. The energy around Killing Goliath grew, and by this time, I confidently had over 300 members and church leaders who not only caught the vision but could communicate it. Notice the key to executing a successful campaign; I got buy-in and support along the way vs. casting vision blindly to a congregation of thousands. In other words, I identified my allies and equipped them with language to communicate the vision.

Principle 3: Place It Where Others Can Read It

The day following Vision Casting Meeting was Sunday, Jan. 16, 2015. It was during this service that I preached a sermon on Killing Goliath. Remember that this was over seven years ago, so we are talking about a time before our stage was adorned with full digital backdrops giving a visual demonstration of the message. Instead, I used two 15-foot cardboard cutouts of Goliath. In an illustration toward the middle/end of my message, we all took figurative rocks and threw them at the cutouts. As we threw the figurative rocks, Goliath fell. The imagery of everyone taking part in this illustration, seeing themselves as capable of knocking down Goliath, painted the picture and laid the groundwork for what came next.

The energy in the sanctuary was high as everyone was shouting and committing to take down the Goliath in their lives. Then, as the praise and worship quieted in the room, I segwayed into how we, as a church, would walk out Killing Goliath and the benefits therein. In other words, I presented the context and the content. See how that worked hand in hand?

After presenting the content of the vision, I shared ways that people could align their support throughout the giving campaign. From top givers to those giving in smaller increments, God gave me a phrase that would be long-standing: "Not equal giving, but equal sacrifice." I explained that this was not something people would have to pay the same day; it was more of a pledge to pay over four years. The timing is imperative because I found that when people are given time alongside a deadline or end date, their giving is more practical and, at times, even increases.

I made sure to review the pledge areas clearly on the mic, and as I was speaking, greeters passed out pledge cards across the sanctuary. The pledge cards explained the giving tiers and showed people different ways to give (i.e., one-time, per year, monthly, etc.). In other words, we presented not only the vision but a clear way in which people could align their support of the vision. I was very intentional about not making one gift seem better than the other, as I wanted there to be excitement in the giving. Hundreds of people submitted their pledge cards that first day, and others spent the following months grabbing pledge cards from the Engage Centers or the front desk during the week.

Our accounting office attached the pledges to each contributor as pledge cards came in. Thus, as people made good on their pledges, our data entry system automatically updated their information. Monthly a report was pulled showing us everything from the total amount pledged, the number of people who pledged, how much was raised, and more. We used this information to guide correspondence with givers, first mailing quarterly letters with an update on their pledge (how much they'd pledged, how much was paid on their pledge, and how much was left to pay). By year two of Killing Goliath, we moved our correspondence online, with people receiving their pledge updates via email. The most crucial aspect of communication was keeping the vision in front of people.

One of my favorite ways to keep Killing Goliath in front of the congregation was by giving meters. In essence, my marketing team took a picture of a giant thermometer and used it as a visual representation of how we were doing with our pledges. I did not show this every Sunday, but I made sure it hit the congregation quarterly toward the end of service and in leadership meetings. People rally around great energy, so as I showed the thermometer, I was sure to do so with excitement, showing the congregation what "we" were doing together.

By year two, Killing Goliath pledges came in less frequently. The excitement that rang in the room a year before when I first announced the vision had a different, slower tune. During this time, I went to God and prayed for direction to reinvigorate the congregation and promote giving without sounding like I was "begging" over the mic. In response to my prayer, God gave me two phrases to share with the congregation: (1) "We give not because we have to, but because we get to" and (2) "What you do for God's house, God will do for your house."

The first phrase, "We give not because we have to, but because we get to," made some of my leaders scratch their heads. Just think: I was in the middle of a multimillion-dollar giving campaign alongside a multimillion-dollar operating budget, telling people God did not need their money. I did not know how the phrase would be received, but I knew what God told me, so I said it with conviction and authority! By the second month of using this phrase during the offering, it became part of the call and response liturgy as I would say, "We give not because we have to," and the congregation would joyfully say, "but because we get to!" It changed the entire giving dynamic; slowly but surely, the pledge numbers increased, and we began to creep up the thermometer. To this very day, we still use these phrases during the offertory appeal.

The second phrase God gave me was, "What you do for God's house, God will do for your house." This was a powerful spin on the old gospel song, "You can't beat God's giving, no matter how you try." Through this phrase, I could share with the congregation the cause-and-effect nature of giving to God. So many people caught hold of this phrase as it was realized that the seeds sown for the church would reap a harvest in our own homes.

During my pastoral anniversary in 2019, my chief administrative officer officially announced that we'd killed Goliath. I can still hear the roars of shouting and excitement in the room. It was not a lone win for me; it was a win for our entire church! In four years, we shifted the church's legacy in a way that would impact generations we were yet to meet.

The assignment of Killing Goliath was a strategic move to do more in the community. The truth is, being debt free was less of a luxury and more of a responsibility because to whom much is given, much is required.

NOTES

NOTES

Chapter 4:
COLLABORATION

Collaboration is a vital component of any successful team. Team members can pull their knowledge and skills to achieve a common goal by working together. When done effectively, collaboration can lead to better decision-making, more innovative solutions, and increased productivity. Of course, collaboration is not always easy. People have different ideas and opinions, which can sometimes lead to conflict. However, team members can overcome these obstacles by learning to communicate openly and respectfully and create a strong collaborative partnership. Collaboration has been a reoccurring theme throughout this book because every vision requires vision carriers.

Vision carriers are people God puts in place to see a vision through. I consider my entire staff to be vision carriers, each with different gifts and talents purposed to fulfill vision. This is why it is essential to get to know your team and those around you so that as vision is given to you,

you have clear direction on how to delegate tasks to move them to completion. This type of divine collaboration requires strong administrative leadership. Now stay with me here because there is a difference between administration and administrative leadership. Anyone with a "type A" or highly organized personality can work in the administration field. However, administration alone does not bring success to an organization. Instead, administrative leadership is required to cultivate the growth and culture needed for organizational success.

Administrative leadership is critical to the success of any organization. Administrative leaders are responsible for setting the organization's direction and ensuring that all members work towards the same goal. They also provide support and guidance to members, helping them to identify and overcome challenges. Administrative leaders must be able to work effectively with other members of the organization, as well as with external stakeholders. They must also be able to make decisions quickly and efficiently to keep the organization on track. Without effective administrative leadership, organizations would quickly become bogged down in bureaucracy and unable to achieve their objectives. As such, administrative leaders play a vital role in ensuring that organizations can function effectively and achieve their goals.

From my experience, I have found three elements of administrative leadership that are directly correlated to collaboration and vision, which I want to take the time to walk through in the following pages.

Administrative Leadership Is An Art

Administrative leadership is an art with an emphasis on creativity and innovation. To be successful, administrative leaders need to be able to master both aspects of their roles. They must be able to develop strategic plans and objectives while inspiring and motivating their team to achieve them. This requires a unique blend of skills and attributes, which can make administrative leadership a challenge. However, those who can rise to the challenge can create transformational change within their organizations.

As an art, administrative leadership is the distinctive and intentional expression of interpersonal communication skills purposed to build and enhance relationships. Like visual art, the art of administrative leadership takes a level of finesse. Examples of the way that I exude the art of administrative leadership include:

- **Children**: I am intentional about interacting with the children and youth of our church. I attend their events and have a strong hand in planning them. What may be most surprising is that I do not have a youth pastor with a church of our size. Instead, I have a team of leaders who meet regularly with my office to plan and execute programming.

- **FaceTime**: Even with a busy schedule, I give my congregation access to me. For example, I never rush out of ministry events unless I run to a service. Instead, I am intentional about using events to get to know my congregation, calling bereaved members, and taking time to get to know each of my staffers — from the executives to those who mop the floor.

Administrative Leadership Is A Science

Administrative leadership is often considered an art, requiring intuition and foresight. However, it can also be viewed as a science with its principles and methods that can be studied and applied. Administrative leadership has its roots in management science, and many of the same tools and techniques used to manage businesses can also be used to lead organizations. By understanding the basics of administrative leadership, leaders can more effectively develop strategies, motivate employees, and achieve objectives. In addition, by applying the scientific method to the study of leadership, researchers can develop new theories and insights that can help improve leadership practice. As the world increasingly relies on organizations to solve complex problems, the need for effective leaders has never been greater. By understanding the science of administrative leadership, leaders can more effectively meet the challenges of the 21st century.

As a science, administrative leadership can be seen as the practical activities one does to systematically organize an organization. I do this in many ways, including yearly vision casting, strategic planning, and our three-month budget planning process. Each of these systems is done in collaboration with other church leaders, drawing on their skills and expertise.

Administrative Leadership Is A Gift

Administrative leadership is a gift. It is the ability to see a problem and find a solution. It is the ability to motivate and inspire. And it is the ability to bring people together to achieve a common goal. Administrative leaders are not born; they are made. They are made through experience, education, and mentorship. And they are made by recognizing the potential in others and helping them to reach their full potential. If you have the gift of administrative leadership, use it to make the world a better place. Use it to empower others. Use it to build bridges instead of walls. And use it to create opportunities instead of barriers. We all have gifts that we can use to make a difference in the world. Use yours wisely.

As a gift, it is essential to remember that administrative leadership is given by God and must remain in submission to the Holy Spirit. Some have compared the gift of administrative leadership to that of a helmsman steering a ship in dangerous waters. The helmsman guides the ship in pursuit of a mission. In the same way, the gift of administrative leadership will allow one to successfully guide a congregation toward a goal. Examples of administrative leadership as a Gift in my life have been:

- Killing Goliath Campaign: *See Chapter 3*
- Leadership Academy: A professional development program to equip church leaders.

When broken down, much of the role of an administrative leader has to do with collaborating and carrying the "burdens" or even hardships of the church. While it is a science, an art, and a gift, it is heavy. So when you think of administrative leadership, think of an ox. To this day, an ox is often used to carry heavy loads. Though the heavy load, it is important to remember that it is not impossible to bear.

There are many ways that an administrative leader can "carry the load." Through my 25+ years of experience in pastoral ministry, I've learned to "carry the load" and made administrative leadership my own. I've done this in three ways that I will share with you: motive, motto, and mentorship.

I. Motive:

What motivates effective leaders? This is a question that scholars have debated for centuries, and there is no easy answer. In general, however, effective leaders tend to be motivated by various factors, including a desire to achieve results, a commitment to their team or organization, and a sense of personal responsibility. For example, an effective leader may be motivated by the challenge of achieving a challenging goal, the satisfaction of helping others achieve their potential or the sense of responsibility that comes from being in a position of authority. Ultimately, what matters most is not what motivates a leader but how they use that motivation to achieve results. Effective leaders can channel their motivation into positive action that benefits their team or organization.

As an administrative leader, one question you must keep in the forefront is this: What is your motive? Take a moment to be truthful with yourself to navigate the answer to this question. As an administrative leader, I make a conscious effort to make sure my motive is always:

- ❖ People over paperwork
- ❖ Devotion over data
- ❖ Ministry over method
- ❖ Human processes over inhumane practices

My motivating force as an administrative leader is keeping my God-given motive at the forefront.

II.Motto:

A Motto is a short phrase that summarizes one's ideas or beliefs. For example:

- ✦ KFC: "Finger-Lickin' Good"
- ✦ McDonald's: "I'm Lovin' it"
- ✦ Chevrolet trucks: "Like A Rock"

Just as these organizations have mottos, you should have a motto that nourishes and cultivates a culture of administrative leadership. My motto is *C.A.F.É* (Commitment, Accountability, Follow Up/Follow Through, and Excellence).

Commitment references one's dedication to a cause. When collaborating with others, knowing the commitment of those with whom you collaborate is essential. Your paid staff or the team closest to you should have the highest level of commitment. This may be seen through their attendance and active participation in required meetings and training; or even their attendance at organization events. In return, I show my commitment as a leader by providing competitive benefits, fair salaries, and opportunities for growth and promotion. On a different level of commitment are Dream Teamers. These individuals are integral to the success of our organization, but they are unpaid. I gauge their commitment to collaboration through their participation in Leadership Academy and service to the ministry. I show my commitment back to them by providing training through Leadership Academy and a comprehensive Dream Team program, including recognition and celebrations. Gauging the commitment of those with whom you collaborate is essential and biblical. In Luke 22:44, we are told that even when faced with the intensity of his crucifixion, Jesus was committed to the process. He intensely focused on the Garden of Gethsemane as he cried blood. Commitment is also very practical in our everyday lives. Think of an eagle. To catch their prey, eagles commit to a process. First, they identify their prey (the task at hand). Then they focus on it with great intensity. And finally, they set out to capture their prey. Eagles never surrender to the size of their prey.

Accountability in collaboration is the act of being dependable. We have several checks and balances in place to ensure accountability at every level of administrative leadership. For example, I would never commit the church to a loan or a contract without consulting my church leaders. Even though I am the CEO and final decision-maker, I am wise enough to understand that administrative leadership is not a silo. Thus, I must know to whom I am accountable (God, my team, and the church). Problems arise when a leader is accountable to no one. Even in Hebrews 13:17, we read, "Have confidence in your leaders and submit to their authority, because they keep watch over you as those who must give an account. Do this so their work will be a joy, not a burden, for that would be no benefit to you." We are all to be accountable to someone.

In my context, there are two levels of accountability. The first level of accountability is for my staff, in which we have yearly evaluations and even a staff-driven approach to ministry. Through this staff-driven approach, every ministry has a staff member who serves as a resource director and is responsible for its growth and sustainability. The second level of accountability is for Dream Teamers, which includes our leadership placement process and Fruitful Feedback. The leadership placement process is used to vet and place leaders. At the same time, Fruitful Feedback is the yearly evaluation given to every Dream Teamer.

Follow up/follow through refers to continued efforts to ensure a task is completed. I often tell my staff, "Inspect what you expect." This reminds them not to fall complacent or depend on others to work just as hard as them. Instead, I challenge them to follow up on delegated tasks to ensure projects are executed excellently. Additionally, we have weekly team meetings when we comb through all current programming, concerns, and events. It is in these meetings that we have hard conversations and problem-solve together. Dream Teamers' follow-up and follow through is seen through pre- and post-event forms. These are virtual documents submitted around events to gauge success and areas of improvement. For clarity, the pre-event form is submitted before each event, sharing the event's details. Then, the post-event form is submitted after the event and shows how close the event matched (or lack thereof) to the pre-event form. These brief forms help us see gaps, innovation, and areas for improvement. Follow-up takes courage, but when done with excellence, it can be one of the strongest parts of your organization.

Excellence is something of superior quality. This is one of the most important elements to measure in collaboration. I can measure excellence with my staff through their project management and stewardship of ministry budgets. I can tell if an event has been executed with excellence by the ease of the event, the attendance, and event the content therein. These are all signs of good project management on my team. However, if an event is choppy and uneasy, I know that excellence was compromised at some point, which is what would then be taken to the staff meeting the following week.

Additionally, I keep a close eye on ministry budgets. Thus, at the end of every year, I sit down with my staff and discuss how they managed their budgets for that year. Let me pause: our chief financial officer checks ministry budgets monthly and oversees every dime spent. Thus, earlier meetings can happen if there is a stewardship concern before my year-end meeting. With Dream Teamers, I gauge excellence by observing their servant leadership at programs and also based on their overall service. For example, do I only see them at church events but not during Sunday worship? At events, are they pleasant and confident or arrogant and unfriendly? All of these are aspects that I look for when gauging excellence.

III. Mentorship:

Mentorship refers to guidance that an experienced person provides. Without mentorship, there is no way I would be who I am or where I am. Keeping this in mind, I promote mentorship within my organization through succession planning. Succession planning is imperative in ministry because it covers leaders and the organization. I know this firsthand because I was part of a succession process. I served my predecessor, Pastor Emeritus Bishop George W. Brooks, as a member of his staff years before I returned as senior pastor. My office was in the church's basement, and I was responsible for the evangelism component of church ministry. I served in that role the best I could, learning along the way through the mentorship of my pastor. Years later, when I was serving as a senior pastor at a different church, Bishop Brooks tapped me to be mentored for my current position. Of course, he could not promise me the position, but he did equip me with everything I would need to have a fair shot.

Knowing the importance of succession in my role was one of the first elements I implemented churchwide by creating the 3-Deep Leadership Model. In this model, every ministry has a ministry leader (#1), followed by a #2 and #3. The #2 and #3 are in succession to fulfill the ministry leader (#1) position at the end of the leadership term or if something happens to the ministry leader (i.e., they get a job in another state and physically leave the local fellowship). Each leader goes through the resource director and the leadership placement process to ensure they are in good standing and are prepared to be a leader within our organization.

Throughout the pages of this book, I have highlighted vital signs of vision from conception to communicating it effectively. However, the next and final chapter brings us to one of the most vital signs of vision: carrying a vision to *completion*.

NOTES

NOTES

Chapter 5:
COMPLETION

Year after year, I meet hundreds of visionaries across the country who have gifts and talents both within and outside of the church and business world. But unfortunately, many of the visions failed to launch because, despite the creativity and clarity in their vision, they failed to carry it to completion. The truth is that a vision is worthless without the ability to execute it. Ask any would-be entrepreneur with a great idea but couldn't get it off the ground. They will tell you that having a great idea is only the first step; what you do with that idea counts. Furthermore, I have deduced that people create vision but don't complete it because (1) they can't manage it or (2) they can't measure it.

Management is achieving organizational goals by working with and through people and other resources. Managers plan, organize, direct, and control an organization's resources to achieve its goals. All organizations need management, whether for-profit businesses, nonprofit organizations, or government agencies. Management is essential for any organization to function effectively. Good management is especially important in a fast-changing environment where organizations must be able to adapt quickly to new challenges and opportunities. The role of managers is to help their organizations be successful. They do this by working with and through people to get things done. Managers must be able to motivate employees, resolve conflicts, make decisions, and provide leadership. They also need to be skilled at planning, organizing, controlling, and communicating. Management is a complex process, but it is essential for any organization that wants to be successful.

I usually teach and preach about management during Stewardship Month at my church. I share various Scriptures in the Bible that show how God gives us things to manage here on earth, from our tithe to our talents. And when teaching on this topic, there is a reoccurring illustration that always seems to shed light on the topic: that of a restaurant manager. You can always tell who the manager is when you go out to eat. Not just by attire, but it is the manager who goes from table to table, checking on guests, engaging in small talk, and providing leadership to other team members. They take pride in the restaurant and a manager, a good manager, uses their influence to guide their team in providing an optimal experience for guests.

Yet to live up to the standard of an effective manager, one must have a myriad of training and skills, including strategy, communication skills, and integrity. These are the same skills needed when managing a vision. A vision without management is simply a dream. When strategy and an effective plan are added, the vision gains wings to fly. You can align a vision with strategy using some of the administrative components highlighted in the last chapter, or you can connect with someone with administrative gifting.

Before becoming the CEO and senior pastor of Mount Zion, I had the opportunity to serve as the chief administrative officer. The CAO is responsible for the overall administration of a company or organization. This includes overseeing the day-to-day operations, developing and implementing policies and procedures, and coordinating the work of the various departments. The CAO reports directly to the CEO or president and is typically one of the highest-ranking executives in the company. The CAO may also have a team of vice presidents or directors reporting to them in large organizations. The CAO is vital in ensuring that the organization runs smoothly and efficiently. Therefore, they must have strong leadership and management skills and a deep understanding of the organization's operations. In the role of CAO, I tapped into my administrative gifting, which has been an essential asset in managing my vision for my professional and personal life.

However, managing a vision is not always easy. The process requires careful consideration of the organization's values, goals, and objectives. Once the vision has been created, it must be revisited regularly to ensure that it remains relevant and actionable. By taking the time to properly manage a vision, organizations can ensure that they remain focused on their long-term goals even as they navigate the ever-changing landscape of business.

The second cause of a vision failing to launch is a lack of measurement. We are encouraged to measure vision in Luke 14: 25-33. Specifically, in verse 18, it reads, " [28] For which of you, desiring to build a tower, does not first sit down and count the cost, whether he has enough to complete it?" In other words, without a measurable vision, it is difficult for any organization to make progress toward its goals. A vision provides a sense of direction and gives everyone in the organization a shared understanding of what they are working towards. Without a vision, it is easy for people to become bogged down in details and lose sight of the big picture.

Additionally, a measurable vision provides a tangible way to track progress and identify where areas of improvement are needed. It can be used as a guide to setting priorities and making decisions, and it can help to keep everyone on the same page. Simply put, a vision is essential for any organization to achieve lasting success.

In the world of business, it is essential to be able to measure progress and results. This is why most businesses have clear goals and objectives that can be quantified. However, another type of vision is not always measurable but can be just as important to a business's success. This is the vision of the future that a company's leaders have. It is the ability to see beyond the here and now, identify opportunities and trends, and make decisions to position the company for long-term success. While this type of vision may not be easy to measure, it is essential for business success. Without it, a company will likely miss out on new opportunities and be left behind by its competitors. So how is vision measured? For me, I use lead and lag measures.

Organizational performance is typically measured by a combination of lead and lag indicators. Lead measures predict future success, while lag measures reflect past performance. For example, customer satisfaction is a lead measure, as it can help to predict future sales. In contrast, revenue is a lag measure, as it captures results that have already been achieved. While both indicators are important, lead measures are often emphasized more, providing a more direct connection to the desired outcome. Companies often invest more resources in tracking and improving lead measures. However, it is important to remember that both measures are needed to get a complete picture of organizational performance.

While it is exciting to focus on lead measures, do not overlook lag measures. When carrying out a vision in my context, I always look at what did and did not work in the past (lag measure). For example, I examine which events, programming, guests, and teachings generated effective responses. An example is a sermon I preach on the fourth Sunday of every September called Follow. Every September is Discipleship Month, meaning I fill the month with teaching and preaching on discipleship. About four years ago, I preached the sermon "Follow;" it resonated with people and effectively communicated their next steps. It was the perfect way to wrap up the month. The following year, I decided to preach the same message, and though the scripture and theme were the same, so many people spoke of receiving an even clearer message from it. So using this lag measure, I continued preaching the sermon every year, and now it is a staple message to close out Discipleship Month.

With effective management and measurement, a vision will be carried to completion. Turning a vision into reality requires building a team, creating a plan, and making things happen. It's not easy, but it can be done. The first step is to build a team of like-minded individuals who share your passion for the vision and are willing to work hard to make it a reality. Once you have your team in place, the next step is to create a plan of action. This plan should identify specific milestones and target dates for each process stage. Finally, it's time to implement the plan and start making things happen. It won't be easy, but you can turn your vision into reality with hard work and determination.

A vision is a timeless seed that will grow and blossom over time. It is important to have a clear understanding of what the vision entails and a concrete plan for how to bring it to fruition. People often allow their vision to remain in the realm of ideas, never taking the necessary steps to make it a reality. To bring vision to life, it is essential to have focus and determination. You must be willing to put in the hard work required to see your dreams come true.

Additionally, you must be open to adjusting along the way. Just as a tree needs water and sunlight to grow, your vision will need attention and care to flourish. However, by carrying out your vision with diligence and perseverance, you can create something beautiful and transform your corner of the world.

NOTES

NOTES

ACKNOWLEDGMENTS

I am so grateful to my beloved family, who encourage me to walk out of my God-given vision in every area of my life.

A special thank you to the best church on this side of glory, Mount Zion Church, where God continues to ordain vision carriers to help me carry His work to completion.

To every entrepreneur, business leader, professional, pastor, and friend reading this book, I pray that you find renewed clarity and strategy for executing your vision. As you align the vital signs discussed in this book with your vision, I pray that you find language and purpose to move your vision forward.

If this book empowered you, I want you to share it with someone and remember to write an online review to encourage other visionaries to make this purchase. Also, I invite you to contact me to let me know how you use this book's strategies to launch your vision. You can reach me directly at Pierceb@mtzbc.com.

If you want to stay connected for updates about future publications and events, check out my website at www.bjp-ministries.com.